Kluwell
My Home Reading™

Green Level

Name: Koral-May Cooper
Teacher: Miss Harvey
Class: Woodpecker Date commenced: 1/9/16
School: St Martins Primary School

Written by Stan Kluzek & Andrew Coldwell

Kluwell My Home Reading – Green Level
ISBN 978-0-9578745-5-8
8th Edition

Published by:
Kluwell Publications
email: info@kluwell.com
www.kluwell.com

Copyright © Stan Kluzek & Andrew Coldwell 1991,
Illustrations Copyright © John Veeken 2015

All rights reserved. No part of this publication may be reproduced, stored in a retrieval system, or transmitted, in any form, or by any means, electronic, mechanical, photocopying, recording or otherwise, without the prior permission of the publisher.

Illustrated by John Veeken
www.johnveeken.com

Using this journal

This journal is designed to be used by the parent, student and teacher. The journal should accompany a student's reading material.
The purpose of this journal is to:-
- encourage regular reading habits (e.g. five nights a week).
- monitor reading frequency.
- provide communication between parent, student and teacher.
- provide a variety of reading ideas for parents.
- stimulate the student to achieve reading awards for every 25 days of reading.

This journal should be used as a record of what is read throughout each week. Saturday and Sunday have also been included.
Provision is made for reading to occur over school vacations and public holidays.
N.B. If a night is missed, your child could read in the morning.

Participating in Reading

Your child does not have to always be the reader to participate in reading.
Reading activities could be:-
a. Reading WITH your child (either taking turns or together).
b. Reading TO your child.
c. The child reading INDEPENDENTLY (aloud or silently).
d. The child MAKING UP or PREDICTING the story.
These variations of reading could be noted in the COMMENTS section.

Date and Title

1. Include a date for each day.
2. Record the title of book, magazine, etc. beside the date.
3. Each recording page is over the period of a week.

Comments

A brief comment is required each night your child has been reading.
Some EXAMPLES of comments are:-
"I thought it was sad when ...."
"It was funny when ...."
"I laughed a lot when ...."
"I read this book .... times."
"The main character was ...."

If NO reading takes place that night, DO NOT write a comment.

For Your Child To Do
Your child has the opportunity to show what they felt about the reading activity they have done.

The faces need a mouth!
Give the faces a smile, frown or just a straight line (hair, ears and other features can be added too).

Weekly Comment
This space can be for a comment(s) from parent(s), student or a teacher to provide feedback on reading progress.
For an example of how to fill in your journal, see the Sample Recording Page on Pg 4.

Number of Days
Remember to keep a cumulative count of the number of days that reading activities take place. The awards throughout this journal depend on you keeping an accurate count.

The Awards
Awards are achieved when a student has read for each 25 nights. Hence, there are 8 awards, which equate to 200 night's reading. There is a final end of year award which allows the TOTAL number of nights achieved to be recorded.
The awards are highly motivational for your child and are a key element of the journal.
REMEMBER that everyone's reading habits are different. Resist the temptation to compare one student's efforts with another.

The Stickers
The stickers in the centre of this journal are highly motivational.
Award Stickers. These are placed on the awards as the student achieves them.
Student Stickers. These can be placed with the Comments section from time to time (see the Sample Recording Page on Pg 4).

Sample Recording Page

Below is an example of a recording page complete with comments and progress. Suggestions for recording your child's progress are included on pages 2 and 3.

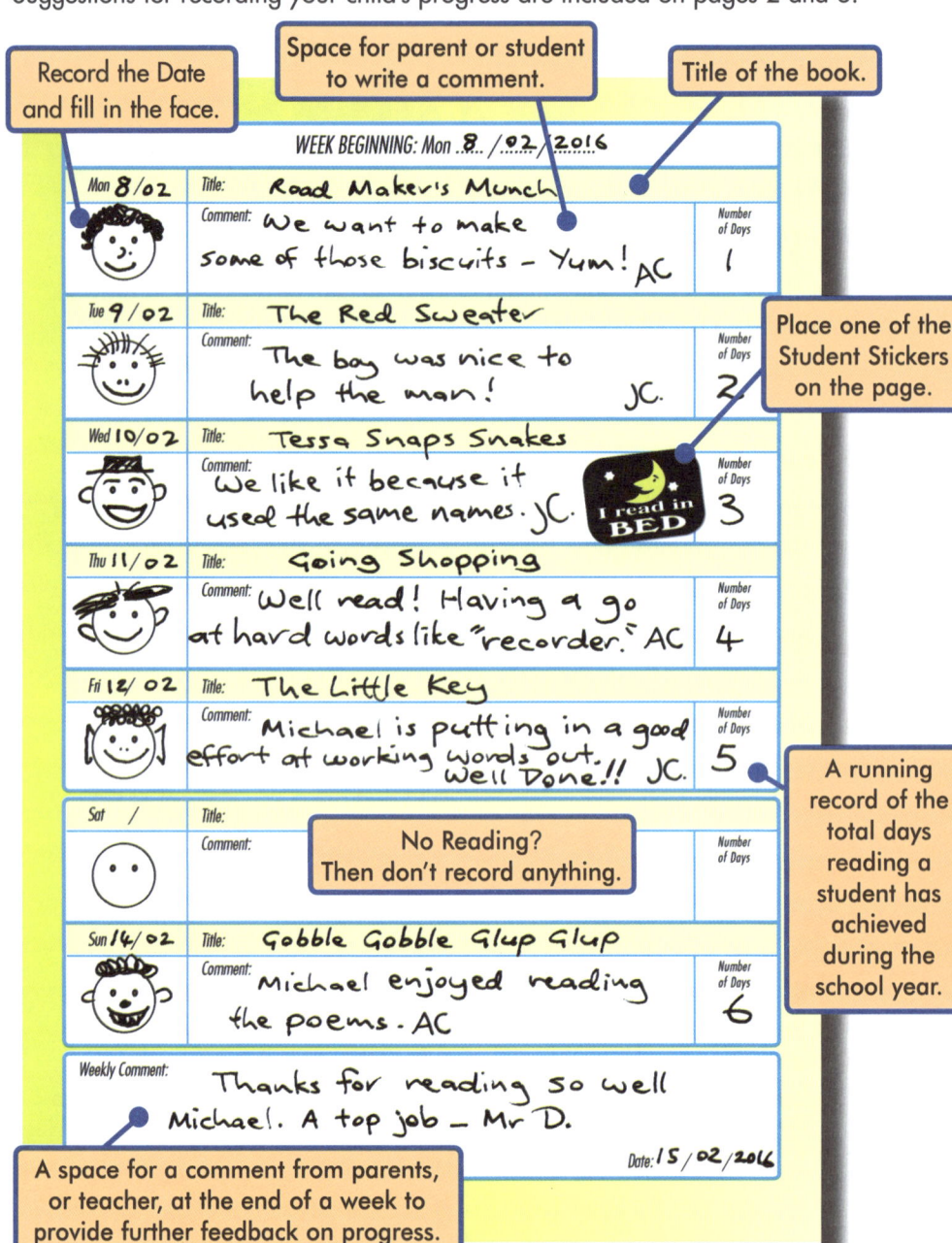

- Record the Date and fill in the face.
- Space for parent or student to write a comment.
- Title of the book.
- Place one of the Student Stickers on the page.
- A running record of the total days reading a student has achieved during the school year.
- A space for a comment from parents, or teacher, at the end of a week to provide further feedback on progress.

WEEK BEGINNING: Mon 8 / 02 / 2016

Day	Title / Comment	Number of Days
Mon 8/02	**Title:** Road Maker's Munch **Comment:** We want to make some of those biscuits – Yum! AC	1
Tue 9/02	**Title:** The Red Sweater **Comment:** The boy was nice to help the man! JC	2
Wed 10/02	**Title:** Tessa Snaps Snakes **Comment:** We like it because it used the same names. JC *(I read in BED sticker)*	3
Thu 11/02	**Title:** Going Shopping **Comment:** Well read! Having a go at hard words like "recorder." AC	4
Fri 12/02	**Title:** The Little Key **Comment:** Michael is putting in a good effort at working words out.!! Well Done!! JC	5
Sat /	**Title:** **Comment:** No Reading? Then don't record anything.	
Sun 14/02	**Title:** Gobble Gobble Glup Glup **Comment:** Michael enjoyed reading the poems. AC	6

Weekly Comment: Thanks for reading so well Michael. A top job – Mr D.

Date: 15 / 02 / 2016

When reading a book you could discuss the following statements:-

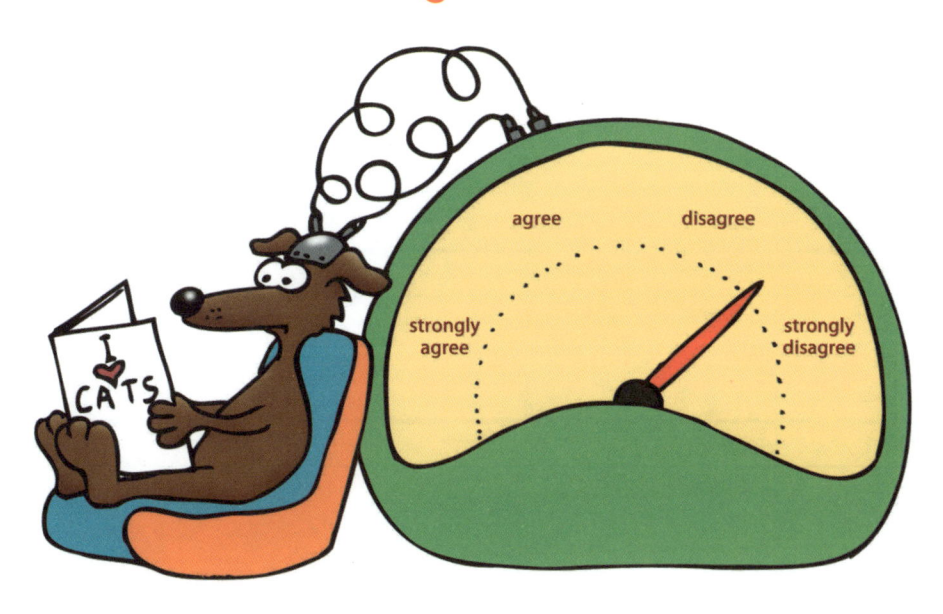

I *enjoyed* reading this book.

| Strongly agree | Agree | Disagree | Strongly disagree |

I would like to read more books by this *author*.

| Strongly agree | Agree | Disagree | Strongly disagree |

I could think of a *friend* that would like to read this book.

| Strongly agree | Agree | Disagree | Strongly disagree |

This book would also be suitable for *adults* to read.

| Strongly agree | Agree | Disagree | Strongly disagree |

This book is suitable for both *boys and girls*.

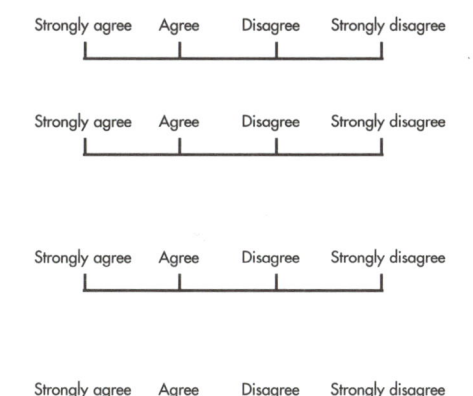

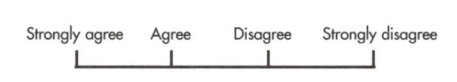

| Strongly agree | Agree | Disagree | Strongly disagree |

| WEEK BEGINNING: Mon 29 / 08 / 16 |

Mon /	Title:	
😊	Comment:	Number of Days

Tue /	Title:	
😊	Comment:	Number of Days

Wed /	Title:	
😊	Comment:	Number of Days

Thu OVO /	Title:	
😊	Comment:	Number of Days

Fri /	Title:	
😊	Comment:	Number of Days

Sat /	Title:	
😊	Comment:	Number of Days

Sun /	Title:	
😊	Comment:	Number of Days

Weekly Comment:

Date: / /

WEEK BEGINNING: Mon ...... /........ /...........

Mon /
Title:
Comment:
Number of Days

Tue /
Title:
Comment:
Number of Days

Wed /
Title:
Comment:
Number of Days

Thu /
Title:
Comment:
Number of Days

Fri /
Title:
Comment:
Number of Days

Sat /
Title:
Comment:
Number of Days

Sun /
Title:
Comment:
Number of Days

Weekly Comment:

Date: / /

WEEK BEGINNING: Mon ...... /....... /..........

Mon /	Title:		
🙂	Comment:		Number of Days

Tue /	Title:		
🙂	Comment:		Number of Days

Wed /	Title:		
🙂	Comment:		Number of Days

Thu /	Title:		
🙂	Comment:		Number of Days

Fri /	Title:		
🙂	Comment:		Number of Days

Sat /	Title:		
🙂	Comment:		Number of Days

Sun /	Title:		
🙂	Comment:		Number of Days

Weekly Comment:

Date: / /

A Suitable Reading Environment

A Suitable Reading Environment should be:-

- Quiet.
- Comfortable.
- Where you can be close to your child.
- Relaxing for both you and your child.
- Free from interruptions.
- Enjoyable, interesting and passionate.
- Full of opportunities to praise your child.

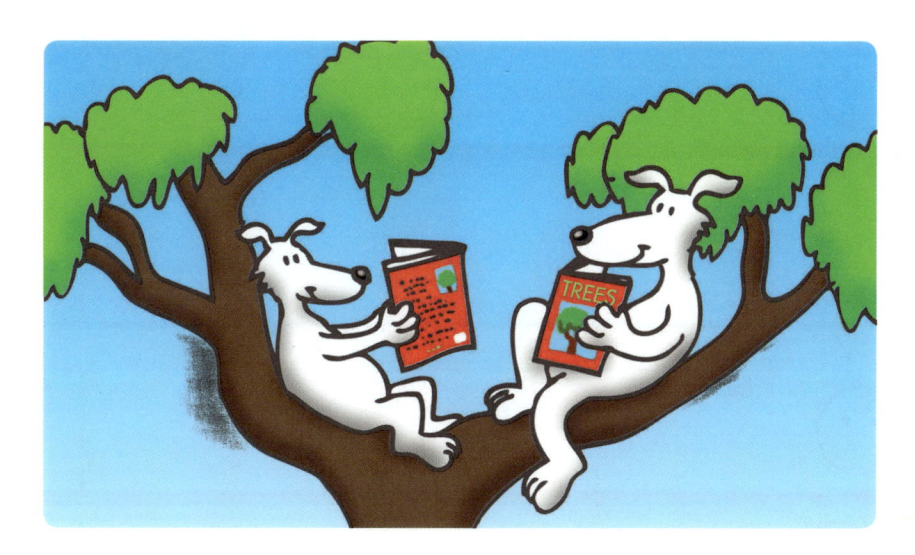

REMEMBER to be seen as a READER YOURSELF.

WEEK BEGINNING: Mon ...... /....... /..........

Mon /	Title:	
😊	Comment:	Number of Days

Tue /	Title:	
😊	Comment:	Number of Days

Wed /	Title:	
😊	Comment:	Number of Days

Thu /	Title:	
😊	Comment:	Number of Days

Fri /	Title:	
😊	Comment:	Number of Days

Sat /	Title:	
😊	Comment:	Number of Days

Sun /	Title:	
😊	Comment:	Number of Days

Weekly Comment:

Date: / /

WEEK BEGINNING: Mon ...... /....... /..........

Mon / | Title:
--- | Comment: | Number of Days

Tue / | Title:
--- | Comment: | Number of Days

Wed / | Title:
--- | Comment: | Number of Days

Thu / | Title:
--- | Comment: | Number of Days

Fri / | Title:
--- | Comment: | Number of Days

Sat / | Title:
--- | Comment: | Number of Days

Sun / | Title:
--- | Comment: | Number of Days

Weekly Comment:

Date: / /

WEEK BEGINNING: Mon ...... /....... /..........

Mon /
Title:
Comment:
Number of Days

Tue /
Title:
Comment:
Number of Days

Wed /
Title:
Comment:
Number of Days

Thu /
Title:
Comment:
Number of Days

Fri /
Title:
Comment:
Number of Days

Sat /
Title:
Comment:
Number of Days

Sun /
Title:
Comment:
Number of Days

Weekly Comment:

Date: / /

READING AWARD

Awarded to

....

for 25 nights reading

signed: ....   date: / /

WEEK BEGINNING: Mon ...... /....... /..........

Mon /	Title:	
😊	Comment:	Number of Days

Tue /	Title:	
😊	Comment:	Number of Days

Wed /	Title:	
😊	Comment:	Number of Days

Thu /	Title:	
😊	Comment:	Number of Days

Fri /	Title:	
😊	Comment:	Number of Days

Sat /	Title:	
😊	Comment:	Number of Days

Sun /	Title:	
😊	Comment:	Number of Days

Weekly Comment:

Date: / /

Be Patient

Do encourage your child to guess what the story is about.

Do praise your child when an idea or word is used that you know will come up in the story.

Do ask questions like:-
"What can you tell about the story from the picture?"
"What do you think will happen in the story?"

Do talk about the start of the story, what happened by the end of the story, the people in the story etc.

Do mention things like:-
The person who wrote the story - the author.
The person who did the illustrations - the illustrator.

Find these people on the front cover of the book.
Where else can you find their names?

Do make sure that whatever your child reads is a complete story, chapter or thought.

WEEK BEGINNING: Mon ...... /....... /..........

Mon /	Title:	
😐	Comment:	Number of Days

Tue /	Title:	
😐	Comment:	Number of Days

Wed /	Title:	
😐	Comment:	Number of Days

Thu /	Title:	
😐	Comment:	Number of Days

Fri /	Title:	
😐	Comment:	Number of Days

Sat /	Title:	
😐	Comment:	Number of Days

Sun /	Title:	
😐	Comment:	Number of Days

Weekly Comment:

Date: / /

WEEK BEGINNING: Mon ...... / .... / ....

Mon / | Title:
Comment: | Number of Days

Tue / | Title:
Comment: | Number of Days

Wed / | Title:
Comment: | Number of Days

Thu / | Title:
Comment: | Number of Days

Fri / | Title:
Comment: | Number of Days

Sat / | Title:
Comment: | Number of Days

Sun / | Title:
Comment: | Number of Days

Weekly Comment:

Date: / /

WEEK BEGINNING: Mon ...... /....... /..........

Mon /
Title:
Comment: | Number of Days

Tue /
Title:
Comment: | Number of Days

Wed /
Title:
Comment: | Number of Days

Thu /
Title:
Comment: | Number of Days

Fri /
Title:
Comment: | Number of Days

Sat /
Title:
Comment: | Number of Days

Sun /
Title:
Comment: | Number of Days

Weekly Comment:

Date: / /

Suggestions to Help Increase Understanding

One way of helping your child to understand what they are reading or listening to is to get your child to ask questions.

So.. when you are involved with reading with your child, try the following:-

1. Before reading takes place, ask your child to think of one question to ask.

2. Your child listens or reads (silently or out loud) thinking about a good question to ask.

3. When reading is finished your child asks their question.

4. You could also ask a question of your child.

5. As your child's questions become more complex you could gradually get them to ask more than one question.

THIS CERTAINLY HELPS WITH UNDERSTANDING WHAT IS READ.

WEEK BEGINNING: Mon ...... / .... / ....

Mon /	Title:	
(face)	Comment:	Number of Days

Tue /	Title:	
(face)	Comment:	Number of Days

Wed /	Title:	
(face)	Comment:	Number of Days

Thu /	Title:	
(face)	Comment:	Number of Days

Fri /	Title:	
(face)	Comment:	Number of Days

Sat /	Title:	
(face)	Comment:	Number of Days

Sun /	Title:	
(face)	Comment:	Number of Days

Weekly Comment:

Date: / /

READING AWARD

READING 50 NIGHTS AWARD

Awarded to
....
for 50 nights reading

signed: .... date: / /

WEEK BEGINNING: Mon ...... /....... /..........

Mon /	Title:	
😐	Comment:	Number of Days

Tue /	Title:	
😐	Comment:	Number of Days

Wed /	Title:	
😐	Comment:	Number of Days

Thu /	Title:	
😐	Comment:	Number of Days

Fri /	Title:	
😐	Comment:	Number of Days

Sat /	Title:	
😐	Comment:	Number of Days

Sun /	Title:	
😐	Comment:	Number of Days

Weekly Comment:

Date: / /

WEEK BEGINNING: Mon ...... /....... /..........

Mon /	Title:	
☺	Comment:	Number of Days

Tue /	Title:	
☺	Comment:	Number of Days

Wed /	Title:	
☺	Comment:	Number of Days

Thu /	Title:	
☺	Comment:	Number of Days

Fri /	Title:	
☺	Comment:	Number of Days

Sat /	Title:	
☺	Comment:	Number of Days

Sun /	Title:	
☺	Comment:	Number of Days

Weekly Comment:

Date: / /

WEEK BEGINNING: Mon ...... /....... /..........

Mon /
Title:
Comment: — Number of Days

Tue /
Title:
Comment: — Number of Days

Wed /
Title:
Comment: — Number of Days

Thu /
Title:
Comment: — Number of Days

Fri /
Title:
Comment: — Number of Days

Sat /
Title:
Comment: — Number of Days

Sun /
Title:
Comment: — Number of Days

Weekly Comment:

Date: /   /

Does Your Child Do Any of the Following?

Tick off

- [ ] Identify base words within other words.
- [ ] Name basic parts of a book.
- [ ] Select own books to read.
- [ ] Read silently.
- [ ] Read often.
- [ ] Read in preference to watching television.
- [ ] Show enthusiasm about what they have read.
- [ ] Show interest in what older people are reading, e.g. brothers, sisters, parents.
- [ ] Read a book as a result of seeing a show about the same topic on television.

WEEK BEGINNING: Mon ...... /....... /..........

Mon /	Title:	
😐	Comment:	Number of Days

Tue /	Title:	
😐	Comment:	Number of Days

Wed /	Title:	
😐	Comment:	Number of Days

Thu /	Title:	
😐	Comment:	Number of Days

Fri /	Title:	
😐	Comment:	Number of Days

Sat /	Title:	
😐	Comment:	Number of Days

Sun /	Title:	
😐	Comment:	Number of Days

Weekly Comment:

Date: / /

WEEK BEGINNING: Mon ...... /....... /..........

Mon /	Title:	
😊	Comment:	Number of Days

Tue /	Title:	
😊	Comment:	Number of Days

Wed /	Title:	
😊	Comment:	Number of Days

Thu /	Title:	
😊	Comment:	Number of Days

Fri /	Title:	
😊	Comment:	Number of Days

Sat /	Title:	
😊	Comment:	Number of Days

Sun /	Title:	
😊	Comment:	Number of Days

Weekly Comment:

Date: / /

WEEK BEGINNING: Mon ...... / .... / ....

Mon /	Title:	
☺	Comment:	Number of Days

Tue /	Title:	
☺	Comment:	Number of Days

Wed /	Title:	
☺	Comment:	Number of Days

Thu /	Title:	
☺	Comment:	Number of Days

Fri /	Title:	
☺	Comment:	Number of Days

Sat /	Title:	
☺	Comment:	Number of Days

Sun /	Title:	
☺	Comment:	Number of Days

Weekly Comment:

Date: / /

Reading Tips for Parents

Praise every effort in reading, especially if your child's confidence is low.

Don't compare your child's performance with that of friends or relatives.

Involve your child in the selection of a story or a book. Ask your child to tell you about something that interests him/her. Use this information when selecting reading material for your child.

We as adults seldom read something that we don't want to, so why force young children to read something they are not interested in?

This is not to say that there is not a time and place for compulsory selection and reading of books. You must balance that yourself.

WEEK BEGINNING: Mon ...... /....... /..........

Mon /	Title:	
☺	Comment:	Number of Days

Tue /	Title:	
☺	Comment:	Number of Days

Wed /	Title:	
☺	Comment:	Number of Days

Thu /	Title:	
☺	Comment:	Number of Days

Fri /	Title:	
☺	Comment:	Number of Days

Sat /	Title:	
☺	Comment:	Number of Days

Sun /	Title:	
☺	Comment:	Number of Days

Weekly Comment:

Date: / /

READING AWARD

REMDING AWARD
75 NIGHTS

Awarded to
....
for 75 nights reading

signed: .... date: / /

WEEK BEGINNING: Mon ...... /....... /..........

Mon /
Title:
Comment: | **Number of Days**

Tue /
Title:
Comment: | **Number of Days**

Wed /
Title:
Comment: | **Number of Days**

Thu /
Title:
Comment: | **Number of Days**

Fri /
Title:
Comment: | **Number of Days**

Sat /
Title:
Comment: | **Number of Days**

Sun /
Title:
Comment: | **Number of Days**

Weekly Comment:

Date: / /

WEEK BEGINNING: Mon ...... /....... /..........

Mon /	Title:	
😊	Comment:	Number of Days

Tue /	Title:	
😊	Comment:	Number of Days

Wed /	Title:	
😊	Comment:	Number of Days

Thu /	Title:	
😊	Comment:	Number of Days

Fri /	Title:	
😊	Comment:	Number of Days

Sat /	Title:	
😊	Comment:	Number of Days

Sun /	Title:	
😊	Comment:	Number of Days

Weekly Comment:

Date: / /

WEEK BEGINNING: Mon ...... / .... / ....

Mon /	Title:	
😐	Comment:	Number of Days

Tue /	Title:	
😐	Comment:	Number of Days

Wed /	Title:	
😐	Comment:	Number of Days

Thu /	Title:	
😐	Comment:	Number of Days

Fri /	Title:	
😐	Comment:	Number of Days

Sat /	Title:	
😐	Comment:	Number of Days

Sun /	Title:	
😐	Comment:	Number of Days

Weekly Comment:

Date: / /

Encouragement

It's so important but easily overlooked.

ENCOURAGING YOUR CHILD IS ONE OF THE MOST IMPORTANT THINGS YOU CAN DO!

Examples like the following could be used:-

- You worked very hard on that word!
- That was fun.
- Great idea!
- You really seemed to enjoy reading that.
- I can tell you are pleased with your reading.
- That's a tricky word but I'm sure you can work it out.
- Knowing you, I'm sure you'll be able to choose something to read.
- You're improving in ....
- Look at the progress you have made.
- I really appreciated you being ready for reading.
- Since you're not happy, what do you think you can do so you'll feel happier?

WEEK BEGINNING: Mon ...... /....... /..........

Mon /
Title:
Comment:
Number of Days

Tue /
Title:
Comment:
Number of Days

Wed /
Title:
Comment:
Number of Days

Thu /
Title:
Comment:
Number of Days

Fri /
Title:
Comment:
Number of Days

Sat /
Title:
Comment:
Number of Days

Sun /
Title:
Comment:
Number of Days

Weekly Comment:

Date: / /

READING AWARD

100 NIGHTS READING AWARD

AWARDED TO

....

FOR 100 NIGHTS READING

SIGNED: .... DATE: / /

WEEK BEGINNING: Mon ...... /....... /..........

Mon /
Title:
Comment:
Number of Days

Tue /
Title:
Comment:
Number of Days

Wed /
Title:
Comment:
Number of Days

Thu /
Title:
Comment:
Number of Days

Fri /
Title:
Comment:
Number of Days

Sat /
Title:
Comment:
Number of Days

Sun /
Title:
Comment:
Number of Days

Weekly Comment:

Date: / /

WEEK BEGINNING: Mon ...... /....... /..........

Mon /	Title:	
😊	Comment:	Number of Days

Tue /	Title:	
😊	Comment:	Number of Days

Wed /	Title:	
😊	Comment:	Number of Days

Thu /	Title:	
😊	Comment:	Number of Days

Fri /	Title:	
😊	Comment:	Number of Days

Sat /	Title:	
😊	Comment:	Number of Days

Sun /	Title:	
😊	Comment:	Number of Days

Weekly Comment:

Date: / /

WEEK BEGINNING: Mon ...... /....... /..........

Mon /	Title:	
😐	Comment:	Number of Days

Tue /	Title:	
😐	Comment:	Number of Days

Wed /	Title:	
😐	Comment:	Number of Days

Thu /	Title:	
😐	Comment:	Number of Days

Fri /	Title:	
😐	Comment:	Number of Days

Sat /	Title:	
😐	Comment:	Number of Days

Sun /	Title:	
😐	Comment:	Number of Days

Weekly Comment:

Date: / /

Encourage your child to identify the words from the list below.

Top 101 - 200 most used words

again	friends	most	small
also	fun	Mr	something
always	has	Mrs	started
another	heard	much	take
any	help	name	tell
asked	here	never	than
away	I'd	new	that's
bed			these
been			thing
before			thought
best			together
boy			told
brother			took
called			use
children			wanted
couldn't	I'll	next	way
dad	I'm	nice	where
door	its	now	which
eat	know	oh	while
each	left	old	white
eight	long	only	why
ever	look	or	who
every	made	other	wish
father	make	really	work
finally	many	red	words
find	may	right	world
first	money	room	year
found	moon	say	years
friend	more	should	your

WEEK BEGINNING: Mon ...... /....... /..........

Mon /	Title:	
😐	Comment:	Number of Days

Tue /	Title:	
😐	Comment:	Number of Days

Wed /	Title:	
😐	Comment:	Number of Days

Thu /	Title:	
😐	Comment:	Number of Days

Fri /	Title:	
😐	Comment:	Number of Days

Sat /	Title:	
😐	Comment:	Number of Days

Sun /	Title:	
😐	Comment:	Number of Days

Weekly Comment:

Date: / /

READING AWARD

READING AWARD 125 NIGHTS

Awarded to

....

for 125 nights reading

signed: ....   date: / /

WEEK BEGINNING: Mon ...... /....... /..........

Mon /	Title:	
😐	Comment:	Number of Days

Tue /	Title:	
😐	Comment:	Number of Days

Wed /	Title:	
😐	Comment:	Number of Days

Thu /	Title:	
😐	Comment:	Number of Days

Fri /	Title:	
😐	Comment:	Number of Days

Sat /	Title:	
😐	Comment:	Number of Days

Sun /	Title:	
😐	Comment:	Number of Days

Weekly Comment:

Date: / /

WEEK BEGINNING: Mon ...... /....... /..........

Mon /
Title:
Comment:
Number of Days

Tue /
Title:
Comment:
Number of Days

Wed /
Title:
Comment:
Number of Days

Thu /
Title:
Comment:
Number of Days

Fri /
Title:
Comment:
Number of Days

Sat /
Title:
Comment:
Number of Days

Sun /
Title:
Comment:
Number of Days

Weekly Comment:

Date: / /

WEEK BEGINNING: Mon ...... /....... /..........

Mon /	Title:	
☺	Comment:	Number of Days

Tue /	Title:	
☺	Comment:	Number of Days

Wed /	Title:	
☺	Comment:	Number of Days

Thu /	Title:	
☺	Comment:	Number of Days

Fri /	Title:	
☺	Comment:	Number of Days

Sat /	Title:	
☺	Comment:	Number of Days

Sun /	Title:	
☺	Comment:	Number of Days

Weekly Comment:

Date: / /

Correcting Mistakes Your Child Makes

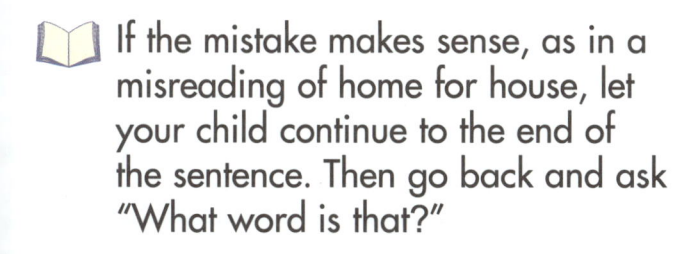

📖 If the mistake makes sense, as in a misreading of home for house, let your child continue to the end of the sentence. Then go back and ask "What word is that?"

ummm...

📖 If the mistake does not make sense, lead your child to correct the mistake by allowing time to self correct.

📖 Reread what your child has said and ask, "Does that make sense?"

📖 Finally, if the meaning is still not clear, look at the word and find familiar sounds such as 's' at the beginning and 'ing' at the end.

📖 Think always of positive strategies when "correcting mistakes".

aaah...

📖 Never use statements such as "That's wrong".

WEEK BEGINNING: Mon ...... /....... /..........

Mon /	Title:	
😐	Comment:	Number of Days

Tue /	Title:	
😐	Comment:	Number of Days

Wed /	Title:	
😐	Comment:	Number of Days

Thu /	Title:	
😐	Comment:	Number of Days

Fri /	Title:	
😐	Comment:	Number of Days

Sat /	Title:	
😐	Comment:	Number of Days

Sun /	Title:	
😐	Comment:	Number of Days

Weekly Comment:

Date: / /

WEEK BEGINNING: Mon ...... /....... /..........

Mon /	Title:	
🙂	Comment:	Number of Days

Tue /	Title:	
🙂	Comment:	Number of Days

Wed /	Title:	
🙂	Comment:	Number of Days

Thu /	Title:	
🙂	Comment:	Number of Days

Fri /	Title:	
🙂	Comment:	Number of Days

Sat /	Title:	
🙂	Comment:	Number of Days

Sun /	Title:	
🙂	Comment:	Number of Days

Weekly Comment:

Date: / /

WEEK BEGINNING: Mon ...... /........ /...........

Mon /	Title:	
😐	Comment:	Number of Days

Tue /	Title:	
😐	Comment:	Number of Days

Wed /	Title:	
😐	Comment:	Number of Days

Thu /	Title:	
😐	Comment:	Number of Days

Fri /	Title:	
😐	Comment:	Number of Days

Sat /	Title:	
😐	Comment:	Number of Days

Sun /	Title:	
😐	Comment:	Number of Days

Weekly Comment:

Date: / /

READING AWARD

READING AWARD 150 NIGHTS

Well done!

Awarded to
....
for 150 nights reading

signed: ....   date: / /

WEEK BEGINNING: Mon ...... / .... / ....

Mon /	Title:	
😐	Comment:	Number of Days

Tue /	Title:	
😐	Comment:	Number of Days

Wed /	Title:	
😐	Comment:	Number of Days

Thu /	Title:	
😐	Comment:	Number of Days

Fri /	Title:	
😐	Comment:	Number of Days

Sat /	Title:	
😐	Comment:	Number of Days

Sun /	Title:	
😐	Comment:	Number of Days

Weekly Comment:

Date: / /

WEEK BEGINNING: Mon ...... /....... /..........

Mon /
Title:
Comment:
Number of Days

Tue /
Title:
Comment:
Number of Days

Wed /
Title:
Comment:
Number of Days

Thu /
Title:
Comment:
Number of Days

Fri /
Title:
Comment:
Number of Days

Sat /
Title:
Comment:
Number of Days

Sun /
Title:
Comment:
Number of Days

Weekly Comment:

Date: / /

WEEK BEGINNING: Mon ...... / .... / ....

Mon /	Title:	
☺	Comment:	Number of Days

Tue /	Title:	
☺	Comment:	Number of Days

Wed /	Title:	
☺	Comment:	Number of Days

Thu /	Title:	
☺	Comment:	Number of Days

Fri /	Title:	
☺	Comment:	Number of Days

Sat /	Title:	
☺	Comment:	Number of Days

Sun /	Title:	
☺	Comment:	Number of Days

Weekly Comment:

Date: / /

Children could be asked any of the following questions when they have <u>finished</u> reading a book:-

Q Did you enjoy the book? Why?

Q How did you choose it?

Q Who were the characters?
- Who was the character you liked the most?
- How could you describe this character?

Q How long did it take you to read?

Q Was there anything about it you did not like?

Q Could you read the part of the book you enjoyed the most?

Q Are you going to read any more books by the same author?

Q Could you make a better ending?

Q Did you come across any unusual words or words you did not know the meaning of?

Q Can you give a brief description of what happened in the story?

WEEK BEGINNING: Mon ...... / .... / ....

Mon /	Title:	
😐	Comment:	Number of Days

Tue /	Title:	
😐	Comment:	Number of Days

Wed /	Title:	
😐	Comment:	Number of Days

Thu /	Title:	
😐	Comment:	Number of Days

Fri /	Title:	
😐	Comment:	Number of Days

Sat /	Title:	
😐	Comment:	Number of Days

Sun /	Title:	
😐	Comment:	Number of Days

Weekly Comment:

Date: / /

WEEK BEGINNING: Mon ...... / .... / ....

Mon /	Title:	
😐	Comment:	Number of Days

Tue /	Title:	
😐	Comment:	Number of Days

Wed /	Title:	
😐	Comment:	Number of Days

Thu /	Title:	
😐	Comment:	Number of Days

Fri /	Title:	
😐	Comment:	Number of Days

Sat /	Title:	
😐	Comment:	Number of Days

Sun /	Title:	
😐	Comment:	Number of Days

Weekly Comment:

Date: / /

WEEK BEGINNING: Mon ...... /....... /..........

Mon /	Title:	
☺	Comment:	Number of Days

Tue /	Title:	
☺	Comment:	Number of Days

Wed /	Title:	
☺	Comment:	Number of Days

Thu /	Title:	
☺	Comment:	Number of Days

Fri /	Title:	
☺	Comment:	Number of Days

Sat /	Title:	
☺	Comment:	Number of Days

Sun /	Title:	
☺	Comment:	Number of Days

Weekly Comment:

Date: / /

READING AWARD

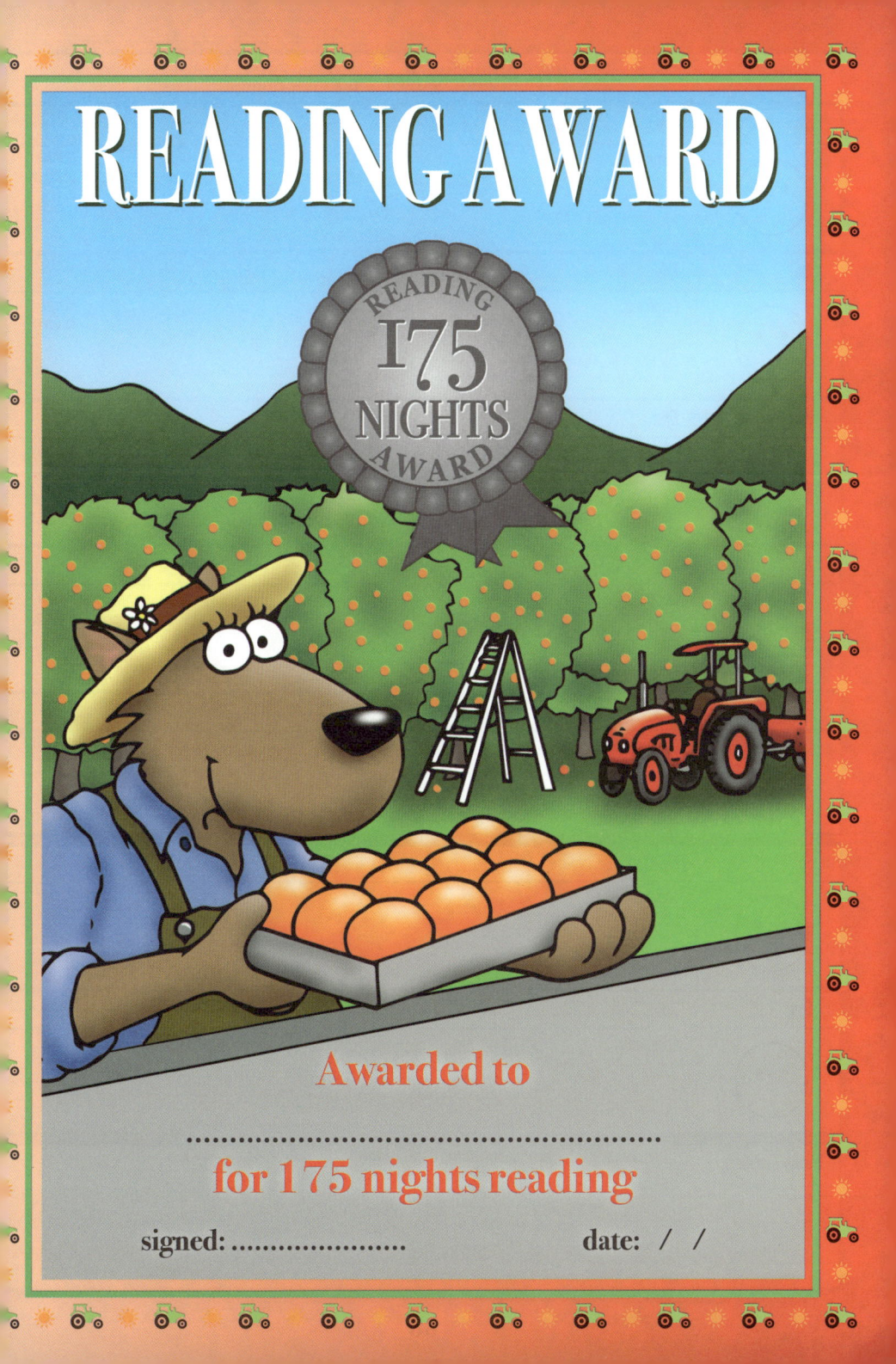

READING 175 NIGHTS AWARD

Awarded to

....

for 175 nights reading

signed: .... date: / /

WEEK BEGINNING: Mon ...... / .... / ....

Mon /
Title:
Comment:
Number of Days

Tue /
Title:
Comment:
Number of Days

Wed /
Title:
Comment:
Number of Days

Thu /
Title:
Comment:
Number of Days

Fri /
Title:
Comment:
Number of Days

Sat /
Title:
Comment:
Number of Days

Sun /
Title:
Comment:
Number of Days

Weekly Comment:

Date: / /

WEEK BEGINNING: Mon ...... / .... / ....

Mon /
Title:
Comment:
Number of Days

Tue /
Title:
Comment:
Number of Days

Wed /
Title:
Comment:
Number of Days

Thu /
Title:
Comment:
Number of Days

Fri /
Title:
Comment:
Number of Days

Sat /
Title:
Comment:
Number of Days

Sun /
Title:
Comment:
Number of Days

Weekly Comment:

Date: / /

WEEK BEGINNING: Mon ...... / .... / ....

Mon /	Title:	
☺	Comment:	Number of Days

Tue /	Title:	
☺	Comment:	Number of Days

Wed /	Title:	
☺	Comment:	Number of Days

Thu /	Title:	
☺	Comment:	Number of Days

Fri /	Title:	
☺	Comment:	Number of Days

Sat /	Title:	
☺	Comment:	Number of Days

Sun /	Title:	
☺	Comment:	Number of Days

Weekly Comment:

Date: / /

READING AWARD

READING 200 NIGHTS AWARD

Awarded to
....
for 200 nights reading

signed: .... date: / /

WEEK BEGINNING: Mon ...... /....... /..........

Mon /	Title:	
☺	Comment:	Number of Days

Tue /	Title:	
☺	Comment:	Number of Days

Wed /	Title:	
☺	Comment:	Number of Days

Thu /	Title:	
☺	Comment:	Number of Days

Fri /	Title:	
☺	Comment:	Number of Days

Sat /	Title:	
☺	Comment:	Number of Days

Sun /	Title:	
☺	Comment:	Number of Days

Weekly Comment:

Date: / /

WEEK BEGINNING: Mon ...... / .... / ....

Mon /
Title:
Comment:
Number of Days

Tue /
Title:
Comment:
Number of Days

Wed /
Title:
Comment:
Number of Days

Thu /
Title:
Comment:
Number of Days

Fri /
Title:
Comment:
Number of Days

Sat /
Title:
Comment:
Number of Days

Sun /
Title:
Comment:
Number of Days

Weekly Comment:

Date: / /

WEEK BEGINNING: Mon ...... /....... /..........

Mon /	Title:	
😐	Comment:	Number of Days

Tue /	Title:	
😐	Comment:	Number of Days

Wed /	Title:	
😐	Comment:	Number of Days

Thu /	Title:	
😐	Comment:	Number of Days

Fri /	Title:	
😐	Comment:	Number of Days

Sat /	Title:	
😐	Comment:	Number of Days

Sun /	Title:	
😐	Comment:	Number of Days

Weekly Comment:

Date: / /

What to read?

Don't restrict your child's reading materials to only books. Provide the chance to read other types of reading material such as:-

Magazines

Comics

Poetry books

Newspapers

Diaries

Reference materials

Atlases

Maps (road maps, street directories)

Instructions for games, machines, etc.

Cooking recipes

Computer adventure games

Letters

Telephone book

Encourage a particular interest by talking and continued reading.

WEEK BEGINNING: Mon ...... / .... / ....

Mon /	Title:	
☺	Comment:	Number of Days

Tue /	Title:	
☺	Comment:	Number of Days

Wed /	Title:	
☺	Comment:	Number of Days

Thu /	Title:	
☺	Comment:	Number of Days

Fri /	Title:	
☺	Comment:	Number of Days

Sat /	Title:	
☺	Comment:	Number of Days

Sun /	Title:	
☺	Comment:	Number of Days

Weekly Comment:

Date: / /

WEEK BEGINNING: Mon ...... /....... /..........

Mon /	Title:	
☺	Comment:	Number of Days

Tue /	Title:	
☺	Comment:	Number of Days

Wed /	Title:	
☺	Comment:	Number of Days

Thu /	Title:	
☺	Comment:	Number of Days

Fri /	Title:	
☺	Comment:	Number of Days

Sat /	Title:	
☺	Comment:	Number of Days

Sun /	Title:	
☺	Comment:	Number of Days

Weekly Comment:

Date: / /

WEEK BEGINNING: Mon ...... /....... /..........

Mon /	Title:	
🙂	Comment:	Number of Days

Tue /	Title:	
🙂	Comment:	Number of Days

Wed /	Title:	
🙂	Comment:	Number of Days

Thu /	Title:	
🙂	Comment:	Number of Days

Fri /	Title:	
🙂	Comment:	Number of Days

Sat /	Title:	
🙂	Comment:	Number of Days

Sun /	Title:	
🙂	Comment:	Number of Days

Weekly Comment:

Date: / /

READING AWARD

FINAL END OF YEAR AWARD

.... NIGHTS

Awarded to

....

for achieving .... total nights reading for year ....

signed: .... date: / /

WEEK BEGINNING: Mon ...... /....... /..........

Mon /	Title:	
😐	Comment:	Number of Days

Tue /	Title:	
😐	Comment:	Number of Days

Wed /	Title:	
😐	Comment:	Number of Days

Thu /	Title:	
😐	Comment:	Number of Days

Fri /	Title:	
😐	Comment:	Number of Days

Sat /	Title:	
😐	Comment:	Number of Days

Sun /	Title:	
😐	Comment:	Number of Days

Weekly Comment:

Date: / /